managing
your
time

Other Studies in A Mom's Ordinary Day Bible Study Series

Jean E. Syswerda is mother to three grown children. A former editor and associate publisher at Zondervan, she was responsible for such best-selling Bibles as the *NIV Adventure Bible,* the *NIV Teen Study Bible,* and the *NIV Women's Devotional Bible 1.* She is the general editor of the *NIV Women of Faith Study Bible* and the *NLT Prayer Bible,* as well as the coauthor of the *Read with Me Bible* and the best-selling *Women of the Bible.*

Erin Healy is the owner of WordWright Editorial Services in Colorado. She is the former editor of *Christian Parenting* magazine and coauthor with John Trent of *My Mother's Hands.* She and her husband, Tim, are the parents of a preschooler.

six sessions

YOU & GOD . YOU & OTHERS . YOU & YOUR KIDS

mom

a mom's ordinary day

BIBLE STUDY SERIES

managing
your
time

**JEAN E.
SYSWERDA**
general editor

written by
**ERIN
HEALY**

ZONDERVAN™

GRAND RAPIDS, MICHIGAN 49530 USA

We want to hear from you. Please send your comments about this book to us in care of zreview@zondervan.com. Thank you.

ZONDERVAN™

Managing Your Time
Copyright © 2003 by Jean Syswerda

Requests for information should be addressed to:
Zondervan, *Grand Rapids, Michigan 49530*

ISBN 0-310-24717-9

Interior design by Tracey Moran

Printed in the United States of America

05 06 07 08 09 /❖ CH/ 10 9 8 7 6 5 4

contents

how to use this study guide

Hey, Mom, are you ready?

When was the last time you did something just for you?

In the joy and junk and memories and mess that is your life as a mother, do you sometimes feel that you've lost some-thing—something essential and important?

The Bible studies in this series will help you rediscover and, even more, enjoy all the parts and pieces that make you a unique person, a unique mother, and a unique and holy creation of God.

The five sections of each individual session are designed to meet a particular need in your life—the need for time alone, for time with God's Word, for time with others, for time with God, and for time with your children. How you approach and use each sec-tion is up to you and your individual styles and desires. But here are a few suggestions:

For You Alone

The operative word here is, of course, *alone.* For moms who rarely even go to the bathroom alone, being alone can seem an almost impossible goal. Perhaps thinking in terms of *quiet* would help. You can do this part of the study in any quiet moments in your home—when kids are sleeping, when they're watching a video, when you're nursing a little one. Any quiet or personal time you can find in your own schedule will work. This part of the study is some-times serious, sometimes fun, sometimes downright silly. It will pre-pare your mind for the other sections of the study.

For You and God's Word

Put this study guide, a pen, and your Bible in a favorite place—somewhere you can grab it at any free moment, perhaps in the kitchen or by a favorite chair. Then, when a few spare moments arise, everything you need is right at hand. Each of the six sessions includes a short Bible study for you to complete alone. (This doesn't necessarily mean you have to *be* alone to complete it! My daughter reads her Bible out loud during a morning bath while her infant son sits in his bouncy seat next to her. She gets her Bible read, and he's content with the sound of his mommy's voice.)

For You and Others

The third section of each study is intended for small groups (even just two is a small group!), but if that isn't possible, you *can* complete it alone. Or connect with a friend or neighbor to work through the materials together. If you function as the leader, little preparation is required; you can learn right along with your fellow mothers. The leader is actually more of a facilitator, keeping the discussion on track and your time together moving along. Leadership information on many of the questions in the "For You and Others" section is included at the back of this book, beginning on page 87.

For You and God

The fourth section of each session will guide you in a time of prayer based on the study's topic. Wonder when you'll find time to do this? Prop this book up in your window while doing dishes. God hears the prayers of moms whose hands are in dishwater! Or take it along in the car when picking up a child from an activity. Or use it while nursing an infant. These times of talking to God are precious moments in the life of a mom. And with all the demands on your time, you need to grab these moments whenever you can. Do also try, though, to find a time each day for quiet, concentrated prayer. Your children need their mom to be "prayed up" when she faces each day.

For You and Your Kids

How great is this? A Bible study that includes something for your kids as well as for you! The final section of each session gives suggestions on applying the principles of the study in your kids' lives as well as in your own. The activities are appropriately geared to different ages and range from simple to more complex.

One Important Final Note

Don't presume you have to move through these sessions in any particular order. The order in which they appear in each study is the ideal. Life doesn't always allow the ideal, however. If you start your study with the last section and then go through from back to front, you'll still be fine. Do whatever works best for you and your schedule and for your treasured little (or not-so-little) offspring.

introduction

Pssst. Mom. Got time for a Bible study?

What? You're too busy? Such is the life of a devoted mom. You love your husband, your kids, your Lord. You do your best every day to serve each of them. You care about your friends, your community, your church. You have gifts others can use, and no shortage of requests to apply them. You try to take good care of yourself, mostly so you can do a better job of meeting others' needs.

You're spending your life doing good things.

Could you be spending your life doing too many good things?

Too many? The question seems outrageous. And yet, why is it so hard most days to get everything done? How is it that a mom's day can become so packed that she has no time for reflection, no time to notice the beauty of God in the unexpected, no time to experience the joy he has built into her work as a mom, wife, woman? How then can a mom's good pursuits leave her feeling fragmented, divided, perhaps even distant from God and her loved ones? How could this be the fruit of her labor?

Somewhere in the depths of your heart, you sense that perhaps it could be true. Perhaps it *is* possible to be doing too many good things.

Maybe it is. What then? In the midst of your busyness, how can you begin to sort out good works from God works? How can you discover what is truly important, not just good?

The six sessions of this study, each broken down into time-friendly chunks, will help you answer these questions—and others:

♣ **session 1: no time for bad feelings**
Finding joy in your work is a gift of God. Are the hours of your day filled with joy, even amid the stress? God says they can be!

♣ **session 2: everything's a priority!**
So much to do, so little time. Even so, it's possible to rediscover the vision and purpose God has for you in the order of your days.

♣ **session 3: a season for every activity**
On the road that leads to the fulfillment of God's dreams for you, you may be tempted to shortcut God's processes. Here's a look at why you shouldn't.

♣ **session 4: the importance of being earnest**
Time management strategies are like diets and financial plans—easy to find but hard to master. Recasting your strategy as an expression of your "sound judgment and discernment" (Proverbs 3:21) can help pinpoint a biblical approach that works best for you.

♣ **session 5: time is pregnant**
Do you see time as a relentless taskmaster, or as a bottomless vessel of opportunity? Your answer to these questions will shed light on the levels of stress you feel during the course of each day.

♣ **session 6: rest for those he loves**
Keeping the Sabbath day of rest is a command, not a luxury. Of all the things on your to-do list, here's why taking a day off should probably be at the top.

Time is a loan to you from God, given to you to invest in his purposes. How are you spending his time? God will show you what he wants if you ask him: "If any of you lacks wisdom," James declares, "he should ask God, who gives generously to all without finding fault, and it will be given to him" (James 1:5). One thing is for certain: No matter how scarce your time may be, the generous amounts of wisdom God will give you will help you use all of it for his glory, not wasting one precious minute.

Not even on "good" things.

no time for bad feelings

 For You Alone

Complete the following statements. Try not to analyze them too much. Just respond honestly with the first thoughts that come to mind.

1. When unexpected events force me to change my plans at the last minute, my first response is usually

    _____ .

2. If I had a quiet hour at home alone and a neighbor I didn't know well knocked on the door, I would probably

    _____ .

3. When I feel overwhelmed by the amount of work I must accomplish in a day, I usually

    _____ .

4. When my children or spouse develop needs that could have been avoided with a little advance planning, I

   _____ .

5. When I say no to a request to take on a project or responsibility because it doesn't seem to be a wise use of my time, I usually feel

   _____ .

6. When I say yes to a request to take on a project or responsibility in spite of not really wanting to, I usually feel

   _____ .

7. When a free hour comes up and I decide to spend it on myself with some indulgence or pampering, I feel

   _____ .

8. It is hardest for me to focus on the task at hand when

   _____ .

Moms can relate to what Jesus said: "Each day has enough trouble of its own" (Matthew 6:34). They often find their hearts bogged down in the swamp of busy days. Guilt, stress, or annoyance are only a few of the emotions that muck up their responses to events like the ones described in the statements above. Yet the heart's desire of most moms is to move gracefully through life as women of God. When they don't, they worry. Inadequacy, failure, and frustration seem more powerful than grace, and they spend their precious days wishing they were better than they are.

But guess what: God's grace is more powerful than your inadequacy, and he wants you to spend the time he has given you on fruitful thoughts and tasks. Each day provides opportunity to become better than you are, but right now you are as good as he needs you to be.

When the "musts" and "shoulds" of life threaten to drown you in Swamp Too-Busy-Days, how can you learn to think differently, to begin to subject these deceptive obligations to the rule of Jesus Christ? Over the course of the next six sessions, tell your guilt and frustration to take a hike, and then get ready for a fresh look at managing your time.

 ## For You and God's Word

The demands on your time often arise out of your commitments to good things—your family, your ministry, your career, your passions and gifts. The Bible proclaims, "Every good and perfect gift is from above" (James 1:17). Of course, not all perfect gifts are maintenance-free.

1. What gifts has God given to you that require a commitment of your time? List three that are especially important to you.

   _____

   _____

   _____

2. Do these gifts primarily bring you stress or joy? Why do you think that is?

3. On a scale from 1 (always) to 10 (never), rank the following statements:

_____ I look at my to-do list each day with a sense of joy and anticipation.

_____ I look at my to-do list each day with a sense of dread and obligation.

_____ I worry about getting everything done that I need to get done.

_____ I enjoy the gifts God has placed in my life.

_____ I am content with my present commitments and circumstances.

_____ I get angry when things I *must* do crowd out time for things I *want* to do.

_____ I worry about the future.

_____ I feel guilty or inadequate whenever I don't have time for things I think are important.

_____ I go to sleep at the end of the day content with how I've spent my time.

Read Ecclesiastes 5:18–20. Write down the verses in the space below. (Writing out a verse often makes you more in tune to its truths than simply reading it.)

_____

_____

_____

_____

_____

_____

_____

4. List three truths you can find in these verses and personalize them. For example, "The joy I derive from my work comes from God alone."

_____

_____

_____

5. What emotions occupy the majority of your thoughts over the course of a busy day?

6. Do the truths you listed above affirm these emotions or contradict them?

Read what the apostle Peter wrote to believers scattered throughout first-century Asia Minor: "Your enemy the devil prowls around like a roaring lion looking for someone to devour" (1 Peter 5:8).

7. What strategies might your enemy use to devour you before you can seize the joy God offers? Identify the factors most often responsible for robbing you of joy.

8. In what ways does God bless you with joy in your daily work? Be as specific as possible.

9. Consider a time in the past when God has enabled you to enjoy your circumstances, even if they were less than ideal. What insights can you apply from this event to help you perceive your emotionally taxing commitments more joyfully?

 ## For You and Others

You work hard, faithfully. You spend time in God's Word. You try to stay organized. Yet still you find yourself wondering why you don't experience more joy in your work—even in work you generally like to do.

Open your discussion by sharing some of your answers to question 7 in "For You and God's Word." Examine together whether the factors that rob you of joy are related to negative thought patterns (for example, a sense of failure when certain tasks aren't accomplished or feelings of inadequacy when you compare your work to someone else's).

As a group, read Romans 12:2 and talk about the following questions.

1. How would you define "the pattern of this world" in regard to work ethic?

2. In what ways do you see yourself conforming (or trying to conform) to this pattern in the way you think about or go about doing your work?

3. Why do you think Paul warned us not to be caught up in the world's patterns? (Look for clues in 1 Corinthians 1:19-21.)

4. What does it mean to you to be "transformed by the renewing of your mind"?

5. How could being "transformed by the renewing of your mind" affect how you look at your schedule and duties?

6. How can you discover this will of God that Paul talks about, especially as it relates to your day-to-day schedule?

The world was made conscious of Protestant time and the so-called Protestant work ethic back in the nineteenth century. Protestant travelers and imperialists imposed their hyperconscious temporality wherever their influence spread. The Protestant clock, not the Catholic cross, was their god. To be prompt and reliable was the surest outer sign of an orderly and responsible inner life.

CLARK BLAISE, TIME LORD: SIR SANDFORD FLEMING
AND THE CREATION OF STANDARD TIME

Our Western culture values promptness and reliability. In social and professional circles we typically affirm people who possess these traits and scold or avoid those who lack them.

7. Discuss how often you think Christians evaluate a person's spiritual life by her promptness and reliability.

8. How does being labeled an "organized" or "disorganized" person affect the way you perceive your own spiritual life? Discuss whether you think this perception is valid.

9. What are "the surest outer signs of an orderly and responsible inner life"? Brainstorm a list of evidence. Use Galatians 5:22–23 as a starting point.

10. In what other ways have you seen the world take biblical principles that apply to work ethic (such as trustworthiness and self-control) and twist them into untruths?

11. What does the world value in an individual's work? Identify a few of the world's indicators of success.

12. How important is wise time management as it relates to finding joy in the gifts (including your work) God has given you?

13. What will it take to transform your mind so that it is not governed by the world's patterns? Speak words of encouragement to one another.

14. What will the reward of such a transformation be?

 For You and God

In her book *The Writing Life,* Annie Dillard notes, "How we spend our days is, of course, how we spend our lives." We know this is true, so to let go of our time management failures doesn't come easily for most of us. If we could only be more organized, wiser, more selective, more disciplined, more . . . anything, surely we could live better Christian lives, surely God would be more pleased, surely we would be more . . . joyful. It usually seems easier to crack the whip than to abandon our guilt.

By now you've had time to consider the relative levels of joy and guilt in your life—and to note that guilt is not in Paul's list of spiritual fruit (Galatians 5:22–23). Throughout the remainder of the sessions, you'll examine how to begin sorting out the triggers for these emotions. And just to complicate things, you'll see that God *does* have expectations for how you spend your time. There are such things as failure, laziness, and poor stewardship of your days. It is possible to disappoint God in the area of managing your time.

But before you go any further, stop and read Romans 8:1, 5–6. Write down verses 1 and 6.

Embrace the truth that Jesus Christ does not bring you condemnation. When you've sought his forgiveness, any feelings of guilt that remain are not from him. Spend time in prayer, asking God to begin conforming your mind to his Spirit and his desires for you. Ask him to teach you how to submit your life to him rather than allow it to be ruled by guilt and the tyranny of the "musts" and "shoulds" of life. Ask him to show you the difference between conviction and condemnation so that you can hear his voice, make the right course corrections, and not be misled by the Enemy. Ask him to fill each of your days with the joy that he promises will spill over out of the good gifts he has given you.

Meditate on this truth throughout the week: Be transformed by the renewing of your mind (Romans 12:2), for the mind controlled by the Spirit is life and peace (Romans 8:6).

 ## For You and Your Kids

Preschool–Elementary

Do you notice a change in your children's behaviors and attitudes when you're feeling pressed by the demands on your time? At different moments—on a restful Sunday afternoon, after a busy day, during playtime, after discipline, and so on—ask your children to draw a picture of how they feel. If they don't like to draw, the clever picture book *How Are You Peeling? Foods with Moods* can provide a springboard for conversation. Talk about what they see in the pictures. Do you see your own emotions reflected in the pictures your children have drawn?

Middle–High School

What dreams do your kids have? This is the age when the stressed-out adults in their lives start emphasizing, sometimes unintentionally, that these dreams have a slim chance for survival in the real world. Invite your kids to talk about their hopes. Consciously seek ways to encourage them, setting aside whatever disappointments or disillusionments you may be carrying. Ask God to help you with this important parenting task of nurturing high hope. Ask God to begin restoring his own dreams for you. Share appropriate information about your own dreams with your children and accept the ways they encourage you.

All Ages

Spend a family mealtime naming activities and projects that bring joy to you as a family. Schedule at least one of these—make sure *everyone* can participate—as soon as possible. Protect the time you've devoted to this event.

everything's a priority!

For You Alone

Place a check next to each item below that has crossed your mind sometime in the past week as *something that needs doing*. Feel free to add others that aren't listed.

- ❑ Find time for this Bible study.
- ❑ Make well-balanced meals.
- ❑ Spend focused time with your children.
- ❑ Go to the library with your children.
- ❑ Read a good book to your children.
- ❑ Read a good book yourself.
- ❑ Volunteer at your church.
- ❑ Volunteer in your community.
- ❑ Volunteer at your child's school.
- ❑ Have a daily quiet time.
- ❑ Spend time in prayer.
- ❑ Keep the house in good order.
- ❑ Notice items are running out before they do.
- ❑ Lead, host, or attend a Bible study.
- ❑ Exercise.
- ❑ Eat well.

- ❑ Maintain a presentable appearance.
- ❑ Complete your "other" job in forty hours or less.
- ❑ Create and maintain family traditions.
- ❑ Call long-distance relatives.
- ❑ Write or e-mail long-distance friends.
- ❑ Put all those photos in a scrapbook.
- ❑ Open your home to guests.
- ❑ Help your child with homework.
- ❑ "Date" your husband.
- ❑ Attend a business function with your husband.
- ❑ Fulfill your husband's sexual and emotional needs.
- ❑ Shop for groceries.
- ❑ Shop for clothing.
- ❑ Shop for gifts.
- ❑ Shop for what you forgot the first time.
- ❑ Help your neighbors.
- ❑ Pull weeds.
- ❑ Stay within the family budget.
- ❑ Manage the family schedule.
- ❑ Schedule or reschedule an appointment.
- ❑ Get enough sleep.
- ❑ Stay current on world events.
- ❑ Stay current on local events.
- ❑ Influence local events for your family's good.
- ❑ Improve your mind.
- ❑ Prepare for _____ .
- ❑ Maintain friendships.
- ❑ Remember important dates.
- ❑ Plan celebrations.
- ❑ Write a thank-you note.

- ❏ Talk to your child's teacher or coach.
- ❏ Monitor your child's activities and friends.
- ❏ Pursue a hobby.
- ❏ Find the best deal.
- ❏ Run your taxi service like a well-oiled machine.
- ❏ Find the school paperwork that was due yesterday.
- ❏ Always be prepared for emergencies.
- ❏ Organize a garage sale.
- ❏ Do laundry.
- ❏ . . . and those dishes.
- ❏ . . . and those bathrooms!
- ❏ Find the best child care.
- ❏ Find the best baby-sitter.
- ❏ Find the second-best baby-sitter when the best gets sick at 5:25.
- ❏ Rearrange your schedule when your kids get sick.
- ❏ Provide snacks for your child's school event.
- ❏ Pay bills.
- ❏ Balance the checkbook.
- ❏ Weigh the pros and cons of schooling options.
- ❏ BE FLEXIBLE!
- ❏ Have another baby?!?!?!
- ❏ _____
- ❏ _____
- ❏ _____
- ❏ _____

For You and God's Word

A mom has so much to do, and each task screams its own importance. When your responsibilities affect the lives of others—

husband, children, family, friends, colleagues, clients—it becomes even harder to prioritize. For those of you who attempt to calculate (and yes, some of you have) the number of hours needed in a day or week to do everything that seems important, the maxim "so much to do, so little time" takes on quantifiable properties. How can you possibly get everything done? Unfortunately, cloning yourself is not an option!

Here's some advice: Immediately stop reading magazines and watching TV programs—as if you have time for either—that offer up lists of important stuff to do that has never occurred to you before. Think of how much unnecessary anxiety you could cut out of your life! In all seriousness, de-cluttering your daily lists so that you can accomplish God's to-do list is perhaps more important than any of your other tasks.

Spend some time reading and reflecting on Paul's words to the Ephesians.

> The bright light of Christ makes your way plain.
> So no more stumbling around. Get on with it!
> The good, the right, the true—these are the actions
> appropriate for daylight hours. Figure out what
> will please Christ, and then do it.
> Don't waste your time on useless work, mere busywork,
> the barren pursuits of darkness.
> Expose these things for the sham they are. . . .
> So watch your step. Use your head. Make the most of
> every chance you get. These are desperate times!
> Don't live carelessly, unthinkingly. Make sure you
> understand what the Master wants.
>
> EPHESIANS 5:8–12, 15–17 THE MESSAGE

1. "These are desperate times!" Paul wrote to the Ephesians (verse 16). Other translations read, "the days are evil." What do you think this means?

2. *The Message* defines "useless work" as "mere busywork, barren pursuits" (verse 11). What kind of useless work occupies your time? Is it easy or difficult for you to identify these kinds of tasks?

3. Why do you think useless work is sometimes hard to give up?

4. How would you evaluate whether an activity that requires your time falls into the category of "the good, the right, the true" (verse 9)?

5. At the end of some days you climb into bed at peace, confident that you've accomplished what God wants. As you recall the last time you felt this way, try to identify something unique about your attitude or approach *that* day as compared to other days.

6. Identify different ways you believe God speaks to you about what he wants you to do.

7. What does it mean to you to "make the most of every chance you get" (verse 16)?

8. "The bright light of Christ makes your way plain" (verse 8). What choices can you make each day to ensure that you stand in Christ's bright light?

9. What choices have you made in the past that move you out of the light and cause you to stumble around?

 ## For You and Others

As a group, read Ecclesiastes 3:9–15 out loud and discuss the following questions.

1. The writer of Ecclesiastes says God has "set eternity" (verse 11) in our hearts. What do you think this means?

2. What does the time you experience here on earth have in common with eternity? Anything? Nothing? Explain.

3. Discuss the impact the truth of eternity could have on your perception of the restrictions and constraints time now places on your life.

4. Is time your friend or your enemy? Why?

5. How does the writer define the "good life" (verses 12–13)? How would you define it?

7. Why is this enjoyment of life easier for some than for others?

8. Which statement most closely describes the way you approach your daily priorities?

❑ Work is what God needs me to do in order to accomplish his will.

❑ Work is something I need to do in order to glorify God.

❑ Work is a gift God gives me for his and my good pleasure.

9. Compare each of the approaches above. What helpful insights do you see in each approach?

10. The writer of Ecclesiastes declares that nothing can be added to the work God does and nothing can be taken from it (verse 14). God has made it this way so that we can revere him. What new light does this truth shed on the importance of your daily to-do lists?

11. What do you believe God wants you to gain from your work?

 ## For You and God

Make a list of everything you need to do today (or tomorrow, if you're at the end of a day). Hold the list and pray over it: "Lord, please make my way plain today. Please show me what is on this list that will please you, and open my eyes to see things not listed here that I need to do. Also, Lord, expose the things that only *seem* important but really aren't. Show me the items that are only barren pursuits so I can do what is truly important to you. I commit my day to you and trust that you will give me every opportunity to accomplish what you want."

At the end of the day, reflect on what God showed you. Write down the things that weren't on your list but that God asked you to do as the opportunity arose. Put a line through those items that turned out to be unimportant or "barren." Make a few notes about what you learned.

If you find value in this exercise, repeat it every day for a week, and see if any patterns begin to emerge. Tell a close friend what you're discovering, and ask her to support you in prayer.

 ## For You and Your Kids

Preschool–Elementary

On certain days—invariably your busiest ones—your children are bottomless barrels of requests. The more they ask of you, the more it seems you must say no. Today when your children ask you for something that will take more time than you think you have available (play a game, take them somewhere, help with home-work, read a story), let the instinctive *no* catch in your throat for a moment and consider the opportunity you have. How can you make the most of it? Find a way to say yes to your child at least once today.

Middle–High School

They need you; they don't need you. In this season of growing independence, it may be hard for your children to express when they really want you around. Watch their signals—you know what they are—and give them the gift of your presence at a moment they might least expect it. You may decide to rearrange your schedule or drop what you're doing as a way of saying, "You are more impor-tant to me than this other thing right now."

All Ages

The next time all of you are in the car together, take turns nam-ing what each one thinks is most important to the other. This car-talk might make you squirm, but your children's honest thoughts on how they see you spend your time could be revealing! (You'll likely learn a thing or two about your children's inner lives as well.)

session 3

a season for every activity

 For You Alone

As you commit your daily activities to God, you may discover that figuring out what will please Christ includes more than you originally thought and takes longer than you imagined. You can be assured, however, that his pleasure is that you be "occupied with gladness of heart" (Ecclesiastes 5:20) each day over the course of your life, as you align your dreams with his and allow distractions to fall away.

Even when you accept that God's plans for you are good and will ultimately be fulfilled, the path from point A to B is often filled with tasks God sets before you that you hadn't planned on. Your heart, steeped in this impatient McCulture of ours, yearns to make things happen quickly, and you may be tempted to shortcut God's processes. But being busier for God does not necessarily prompt him to change his timetables. He created the seasons of the world and similarly governs the seasons of your life. Never forget: "There is a time for everything, and a season for every activity under heaven" (Ecclesiastes 3:1).

Taking some time for quiet reflection, draw or describe this present time in your life as a physical season (spring, summer, fall, winter). Are you satisfied with the season you're in? Do you long to be in a different season? Why? What do you love most about this season? What do you dislike?

For You and God's Word

The apostle Peter once wrote, "With the Lord a day is like a thousand years, and a thousand years are like a day" (2 Peter 3:8). We can all laugh and say we've been in seasons that feel a thousand years long. Though Peter is speaking of the timing of Christ's return, his admonitions about holy living can help form your attitude toward the days and seasons of your life. As you spend some time reading from Peter's letter, consider how you can always be prepared to please your Lord "in season and out of season" (2 Timothy 4:2).

1. Read 2 Peter 3:8–15. Write down verse nine here:

Maybe it is human pride that makes you feel that waiting for the Lord's timing means *you* have to be patient with God. But Peter says, "He is patient with you" (verse 9).

2. In what specific ways is God patient with you?

3. According to this passage, why does God choose to be patient with you?

4. What does God's patience tell you of God's love for you?

5. Peter asks his readers, "Since everything will be destroyed in this way, what kind of people ought you to be?" (verse 11). As you think about God's amazing love for you and his earnest desire that you be saved from destruction, formulate your answer to Peter's important question.

A wise pastor once said, "When you don't know what to do next, keep doing the last thing God told you to do."

6. What has God asked you to do in this season of your life? (If you're in between seasons right now, answer the question as it pertains to your most recent season.)

7. Motherhood is a season of varying demands. Which of these demands are most urgent for you right now?

8. Read Matthew 24:45–46. If Jesus were to return today, what would he find you doing?

9. Name three responsibilities you presently have that you can say with certainty God wants you to accomplish in this season.

10. Peter suggests we should not be merely spotless and blameless, but also at peace with the Lord (verse 14). What distractions rob you of that peace? Are they the same distractions that rob you of joy, which you identified in "For You and God's Word" in session 1?

11. What adjustments do you need to make to your priorities in this season of your life?

12. List three achievable, measurable things you can do this week to begin making those adjustments. (For example, "I will take my child to the park Thursday instead of cleaning the hall closet.")

For You and Others

Before meeting together, refresh your memory of Joseph's story by reading Genesis 37 and Genesis 39–41.

Can you remember being young (or perhaps just energetic!) and dreaming big dreams as you looked out on God's world full of anticipation? Can you imagine how Joseph felt as he reflected on the dreams God had given him (37:5–11) and then watched them slip from the realm of possibility? Never imagining that he could lose his status as favored son — at least not in the way he expected — Joseph was betrayed by his brothers (37:12–24), sold into slavery (37:25–36), accused of a crime he did not commit, and imprisoned (39:7–20).

1. You can think of Joseph's life in terms of seasons. Name the seasons of his life based on these passages:

   Genesis 37:12–24 Season of _____

   Genesis 37:25–36 Season of _____

   Genesis 39:7–20   Season of _____

   Genesis 41:41–43 Season of _____

From this side of history, it's easy to see how God moved Joseph through these seasons toward the fulfillment of his dreams. But Joseph's limited point of view must have caused him to be confused by the apparent contradictions between his dreams and his declining circumstances.

2. As a group, discuss how you might have responded to these contradictions if you had been in Joseph's sandals.

3. Scripture doesn't say much about Joseph's inner life (for example, whether he questioned God's intentions or worried about the future). However, what do his outward actions tell you about his feelings?

4. What is unique about the way Joseph responded to his circumstances?

5. Read Genesis 39:2-5; 39:21-23; and 41:39-40. Why did Joseph receive favor in each of his seasons?

6. Do you think the Lord was with Joseph because Joseph was faithful to God or because no person can foil God's plans? Discuss your answers and then personalize them.

7. What responsibilities did God give to Joseph in each season (37:12-14; 39:4-6; 39:22-23; 41:41)?

8. What might Joseph have risked by trying to achieve the promise of his dreams in his own time rather than by living righteously in each season?

9. What do you risk by ignoring the responsibilities God has given you in any particular season?

10. What character traits were developed in Joseph by his troubles?

39:3 _____

39:9-10 _____

40:12, 18 _____

41:16 _____

41:39 _____

41:57 _____

As you conclude your time, encourage one another by naming the fruits you see in each other's lives as a result of faithful living, regardless of the season.

For You and God

No matter what season you find yourself in, God gives you access to the source of life, peace, and strength at all times. When you feel drained dry by your daily efforts or overcome with worry because you can't figure out what you really should be doing, God's Word will water your soul and bring life to your heart.

If reading the Bible has become just another item on your chock-full to-do list, ask God to fill you with a hunger for him and a delight in his Word—and he will do it. Every single one of your days was ordained by God even before you were born (Psalm 139:16), and he thinks of you with love and longing. He wants you to want to delight in him!

Take your Bible and read Psalm 1:1–3 slowly, remembering that it is poetry. Close your eyes and imagine yourself as a tall, broad tree. The day is hot and people are coming to you for shade. They're plucking your fruit and picking at your bark while they eat. The breeze disappeared early in the morning. The sun is beating down, and you are tired. But you are planted on the shore of a deep river, and in the oppressive heat you consider how refreshing and peaceful the river looks. You think you can muster enough energy to stretch out your roots toward its underground springs. Maybe. You stretch. Nothing. You try again. Once more. The tiniest tip of your roots touches the cool water, soaking it in. You stretch further and find more, soaking it in, letting it rush up—up and outward to the tips of your thirsty leaves. You will not wither today. No, you will not wither, not even in winter.

Commit Psalm 1:1–3 to memory and ask God to keep your delight in him firmly rooted.

 ## For You and Your Kids

Preschool–Elementary

Begin a bedtime tradition of asking your children, "What was the saddest, hardest, worst part of your day today?" and "What was the happiest, easiest, best part of your day today?" Begin to plant the idea in their hearts that God is always with them—in both the sorrow and joy of their days.

Middle–High School

Kids grow up quickly enough, but most want to grow up even faster. As your kids yearn for the future ("when I can date," "when I can drive," "when I can go to college"), support them in experiencing and savoring the big and small joys unique to the season of youth. Facilitate youthful fun that suits their interests. Help them research local opportunities that may not be immediately obvious. Think creatively with them about the here-and-now. Celebrate achievements, milestones, and even physical changes with a memento they can keep—a photo or video, a handwritten card from you, news clippings, and so on.

All Ages

Have everyone pitch in to create a family scrapbook or time capsule to commemorate this season of your children's ages and stages and of your family's growth. You could make this a onetime event or an annual tradition. Take advantage of other opportunities to celebrate the seasons of your family's life. Spend an evening together watching home videos, flipping through a photo album, drafting a family newsletter, or updating your clan's website.

the importance of being earnest

 For You Alone

You know the maxim: "If you fall off a horse, the best thing to do is get back on again." But what do you do if the horse keeps bucking you off? Could finding another horse be a good idea?

For most people, time management strategies, like diets or financial plans, are easy to find but hard to master. You have an infinite number of options, from collecting scrap-paper reminders to attending PDA (personal digital assistant) seminars. But finding the strategy that suits you best is tricky. Thrown off course time and again either by a flaw in the plan or a flaw in you, you become discouraged.

Check which time management plan best fits your present strategy:

- ❑ I go through several stacks of to-do lists daily.
- ❑ I look at what I scribbled on a notepad yesterday.
- ❑ I'm too busy to plan anything.
- ❑ I just do the first thing that looks like it needs doing.
- ❑ Planning? What's that?
- ❑ I plan my day in my mind, then tackle each task in order.
- ❑ I spend time each evening with my PDA, planning the next day.
- ❑ I collapse completely at the thought of a PDA.

- ❏ What's a PDA?
- ❏ I write things on a huge calendar on the kitchen desk/refrigerator/wall.
- ❏ I make notes of what needs to be done and then don't do them.
- ❏ I'm usually pretty organized about my day—usually.
- ❏ How can anyone with little kids underfoot really plan anything?
- ❏ Oops! Can't discuss this right now. Someone just threw up on my planner!

Check how you measure the success of a time management strategy:

_____ By how much it helps me accomplish

_____ By how much control it provides me

_____ By how much peace it brings me

Do you think these three measurements are equally valid, or do you think they can be ranked in order of importance? If you think they can be ranked, in what order would you put them?

Conclude your time alone by examining your view of time management. Do you see it as a spiritual discipline, as a human construct that has nothing to do with God, or as something in between? Do you see the order of your days as something you can control, something you can merely influence, or something you must leave entirely to God?

Rather than fall off the time management horse again and again, see if you can corral a tamer horse. The next three sections of this session will explore different aspects of finding some balance in your time management strategies.

 ## For You and God's Word

Do you long to hear the Lord say, "Well done, good and faithful servant! You have been faithful with a few things; I will put you in charge of many things. Come and share your master's happiness!"

(Matthew 25:21). A good and faithful servant works hard, ever a diligent ant (see Proverbs 6:6–7), applying herself to whatever God sets before her. She knows what the Lord wants and does it.

As a busy mom, you may feel on occasion that you've been put in charge of many things before you've been able to gain mastery over the little stuff of life. You don't have to be told to snap out of sluggishness; if anything, you'd welcome an army of ant assistants to help you through each day. You think you know what God wants, but you're just not sure how to get it all done. In lieu of extra help, how can you allow *God* — not the tyranny of the urgent — to govern your days?

1. Read Proverbs 3:21–22 and copy the verses in the space below.

2. Think of time as a boundary, as a limitation around the things that must be accomplished. How would you define what it means to have "sound judgment and discernment" (verse 21) in the context of living within such a boundary? (For example, "I must balance responsibilities that are urgent with responsibilities that require my long-term attention.")

3. Now think of time as an open field of opportunity, a chance to choose to do certain things you might not otherwise be able to accomplish. How does thinking about time in this way change or add to your definition of "sound judgment and discernment"?

4. Do you think of time more often as a boundary or an opportunity? Why?

5. Identify the distractions that put sound judgment out of reach. In other words, what events, people, or ideas derail your time management strategies?

6. Do you believe you are more often derailed because the Enemy is committed to your failure or because your sound judgment may not be in alignment with God's will for you?

7. How can you ensure that your judgment and discernment are biblically sound and reflect God's good purposes in your life?

8. When you wear a piece of jewelry that has special beauty or sentimental value, how does it affect your perception of yourself? Does it make you feel more beautiful? Part of a family? Valued or loved by the person who gave it to you? Consider sound judgment and discernment as "life for you, an ornament to grace your neck" (verse 22). How will possessing sound judgment as you order your days affect the way you feel about yourself? About your relationship with God?

For You and Others

How many of you have learned that time management plans sometimes merely replace one bondage with another? Rather than being bound to laziness or aimlessness, you find yourself bound to the exhausting weight of "if onlys." "If only I could get all this done!" "If only my child hadn't gotten sick!" "If only I could just perfect this system!" Days approached strategically can be just as tyrannical as those attacked without a plan.

In your group, share your answers to the (admittedly silly) quiz found in "For You Alone." Then discuss these questions:

1. How much does your time management strategy rule you?

2. How would you describe your strategy's role? Is it a police officer, a judge, or a friendly guide?

3. Identify ways you can allow God to have as much authority over your day as the goals you've set.

Read James 4:13-16.

4. Is it wrong to set goals and plan ahead (verse 13)?

5. In what way is making bold plans a form of boasting (verse 16)? Why is such boasting "evil"?

6. One look at your calendar will reveal what will happen tomorrow, won't it? What, then, does James mean when he says, "Why, you do not even know what will happen tomorrow" (verse 14)?

7. How are you like a "mist" (verse 14)?

8. How does thinking of yourself as a mist affect the way you feel about the significance of your responsibilities?

9. How might prefacing your plans with "If it is the Lord's will" (verse 15) influence the stress you experience on any given day?

10. It's one thing to say "If it is the Lord's will" and quite another to consciously and completely surrender your plans to God. Think together about some practical ways to *surrender* your plans even while using them as a guide for each day.

11. By a show of hands, identify which group members consider themselves to be disciplined time managers—by no means perfect, still struggling with getting things done, but more inclined to be using some sort of strategic approach to daily life.

Which consider themselves to be a little more freewheeling in their approach to life—finding project planners or PDAs stressful or binding, preferring to stay flexible, tackling responsibilities while making key decisions based on what each day brings?

12. Share with each other what you see as the advantages of your particular approach to time and planning. What are the disadvantages or flaws? What do you wish you could do differently, more easily? Let people from both camps discuss.

Whether you're inclined to be lazy or in perpetual motion, chances are you're familiar with the hardworking ant.

> You lazy fool, look at an ant.
>   Watch it closely; let it teach you a thing or two.
> Nobody has to tell it what to do.
>   All summer it stores up food;
>   at harvest it stockpiles provisions.
>
> PROVERBS 6:6–8 THE MESSAGE

13. Have you ever considered this ant's motivation? What motivates it to store up and stockpile?

14. What might the ant's instincts, set into motion by its Creator, teach you about balance in your own life?

15. How do you define success in your planning? Is it getting all the entries on your to-do list checked off? Or is it sometimes dumping the to-do list and doing what you think God is calling you to do on a particular day? Discuss.

16. It's pretty easy to give the "right" answer to the question above. But how hard do you find it to set aside your to-do list and instead concentrate on something you think God would rather you do?

17. To-do lists typically don't include things like "play with the kids," or "talk to my husband." How do you blend a list of things that need doing with the serendipity of enjoying important moments with your family?

 ## For You and God

To plan or not to plan—that is the question. After spending time on this tricky issue, you may be confused about the strategies God would like you to use—or abandon—in approaching each day. Perhaps each day will require something new or different from you. But don't worry. "Who of you by worrying can add a single hour to his life?" Jesus once asked. Then he went on, "For the pagans run after all these things, and your heavenly Father knows that you need them. But seek first his kingdom and his righteousness, and all these things will be given to you as well. Therefore do not worry about tomorrow, for tomorrow will worry about itself. Each day has enough trouble of its own" (Matthew 6:27, 32–34).

Tomorrow will worry about itself. This word from Jesus is a far cry from Scarlett O'Hara's careless procrastinations: "I'll think about it tomorrow." Rather than dodge life's realities Scarlett-style or become consumed by your preoccupation with worry, you can find peace in the truth that your Father knows what you need, and it wouldn't occur to him not to meet those needs. His love for you is beyond comprehension.

"The time is short," Paul wrote to the Corinthian church. "This world in its present form is passing away. I would like you to be free from concern" (1 Corinthians 7:29, 31–32). Can you imagine living free from concern, free from worry? According to God's Word, it is possible.

With Jesus' promises resonating in your heart, you can go to God in prayer and give him the authority to be your only Master. Ask him to free you from the bondage of rigid planning or laziness, or from bondage of any form resulting from your lack of trust in him. Ask him to give you sound judgment and discernment, so that the troubles of each day no longer derail you but direct you closer to God.

 ## For You and Your Kids

Preschool–Elementary

Kids whose days follow a certain rhythm—a comfortable routine—generally feel more secure and less anxious. Note your child's personal rhythm. (For example, is your daughter a morning person, or does she wake up slowly? Does your son need time to wind down and regroup after school?) Look for ways to blend each child's personal rhythm into familiar music that makes sense for your whole family.

Middle–High School

What critical disciplines or responsibilities are most difficult for your child to master? Homework? Chores? Being on time? Keeping promises? Begin with just one area your child wants to improve, and together develop a strategy to make it happen. Make goals measurable, focused, and short-term. For example, redefine or designate chores so that they match your child's strengths and are realistic in light of daily schedules. Allow at least two weeks for a new approach before reevaluating it. Reward successes. Make yourself a part of the solution by resolving not to foil the partnership efforts. For example, if you've agreed to take care of your own paperwork while your teen is doing homework, don't bail by chatting on the phone.

All Ages

Affirm the importance of each family member's interests, values, and time by creating a family calendar that includes lessons, practices, athletic events, school and church functions, holidays, and other commitments. Younger ones can help decorate with special-event stickers; each family member can use a different color pen, and so on. Keep in mind that it will require give-and-take, grace, mutual respect, and even sacrifices so that the entire family can support one another without starting a war in the process. Keep in mind your family's season and priorities, regularly evaluating particular commitments and desires.

time is pregnant

For You Alone

Did you read this session's title and think to yourself, *Thank goodness it's* time *that's pregnant and not me?*

Let's briefly revisit your general attitudes toward time, which you focused on in session 1. (Perhaps by now they may have even changed a bit.) Complete the sentence "Time is . . ." with the words or phrases that best capture the way you feel (for example, "Time is precious," "Time is short," and so on.

Time is _____

Time is _____

Time is _____

Time is _____

Time is _____

Examine your perceptions in light of the interruptions, yanking, pulling, and twisting your plans can go through in a mom's ordinary day. How does your mind-set toward time affect your reactions to the multitude of unforeseen events that crop up during a normal day?

For You and God's Word

Western culture perceives time *chronologically*—generally valuing time as a commodity, something to be measured and counted (a definite number of hours available in a day, for example). We habitually quantify time: "Time is money"; "time is scarce." Many other cultures see time differently—something that's natural, that passes but needs little notice, that certainly doesn't require counting. To take an extreme example, the Hopi Indian tribe in the southwestern part of the United States has no tense in the verb structure of their language, no sense of time as we understand it in their language or culture. Can you picture your life without a sense of time and its peculiar burden? Hard to do, isn't it?

1. Have you ever stopped to consider how God views time? What do Psalm 90:4 and 2 Peter 3:8 have to say about God's view of time?

   Read Proverbs 16:1–4. Write verse 3 down here.

2. No matter how wonderful your plans and intentions, they must eventually give way to God's. Do you make a habit of setting your plans before God for his approval? Why or why not?

3. What plans do you hold dear that are hard for you to commit to the Lord? What do you fear will happen if you commit your plans to him? What does verse 3 say will happen if you commit your plans?

4. Recall an occasion when the pressures of chronological time (a deadline, a competition, an impulse, a sudden change of circumstance) compelled you to forge ahead with a plan you knew (or eventually discovered) was outside of God's will. What happened?

5. How did God work out "everything for his own ends" (verse 4) in this occasion?

6. Many people speak of time as something that belongs to them, such as "It's not worth my time" or "I only have time for _____ ." How would your speech change if you believed that time is something that belongs to God? How might your thinking change?

7. In *Life-Defining Moments,* James Emery White urges readers to consider time in a *kairos* sense rather than a chronological sense: "*Kairos* speaks to the quality and content of time itself, independent of its actual length. . . . *Kairos* is time filled with opportunity, a moment pregnant with eternal significance and possibility. It is a point of time that demands action, a space of time in which life-determining decisions are made." If you could believe that God does fill time "with opportunity . . . in which life-determining decisions are made," would it be easier or more difficult for you to commit your plans to the Lord? Why?

8. Consider the following perspectives of time in comparison to the list you made in "For You Alone":

- Time is God's commodity.
- Time is on loan to you.
- Time is pregnant with opportunity.

What does your list reveal about your fears as they relate to time? How could this alternative list positively affect your day-to-day decisions and activities?

For You and Others

"Every moment God is giving is precious," Steven Curtis Chapman sings in "Next 5 Minutes," from his album titled *Speechless*. "There will never be another 'right now.'" Once an opportunity has passed, that exact moment can't be recovered.

Read Galatians 6:9–10 and Colossians 4:5–6.

1. When God provides you with "opportunities" (try not to look at them as interruptions), what is often the nature of these opportunities?

2. Why do you think you are encouraged in these verses to be on alert for opportunities that positively affect others?

The word "opportunity" in Galatians 6:10 is derived from the Greek word *kairos.* Consider James Emery White's definition: "*Kairos* speaks to the quality and content of time itself, independent of its actual length."

3. Do you often/usually/never evaluate your opportunities in terms of how much time you have? If you answered often or usually, how can you begin evaluating opportunities in terms of "quality and content" rather than merely chronological time? Discuss.

The word "opportunity" in Colossians 4:5 is derived from the Greek word *exagorazō,* which means "to buy up," "to redeem," or "to improve opportunity."

4. Brainstorm a list of actions you could take to enhance your opportunities to interact with nonbelievers.

5. Take turns talking about a particular *kairos* moment—a pregnant moment—you experienced (recently or in the past) that involved another person. What opportunities were presented to you in that moment? What did you choose? (Missed opportunities are fair play for discussion, too!)

As your session draws to an end, read together 2 Corinthians 8:7, 12. As God presents you with opportunities to give of your time to others, remember what Paul declares in verse 12: *Whatever* you have to give—big or small, significant or insignificant—is acceptable.

6. According to these verses, how does God measure your giving?

7. How do you as a believer tend to measure your giving?

8. Name specific ways you can encourage each other to "excel in this grace of giving" according to what one has and not according to what the next woman has.

9. Talk as specifically as possible about gifts you've seen each woman in the group give to others (to you, too), and thank each for her obedience to Christ in that area.

 ## For You and God

God has offered an incredible promise to those who give generously in moments of opportunity: "Whoever sows sparingly will also reap sparingly, and whoever sows generously will also reap generously. Each man should give what he has decided in his heart to give, not reluctantly or under compulsion, for God loves a cheerful giver. And God is able to make all grace abound to you, so that in all things at all times, having all that you need, you will abound in every good work" (2 Corinthians 9:6–8).

As in every other area of your life, when it comes to time and opportunity, God will provide you with all you need, including clear vision to notice the opportunities and the resources to make the most of each one.

Spend time today praising God for his amazing grace and provision. Express your pleasure in being used to minister to others, and thank him for whatever abundance he has put into your life and is allowing you to share. Ask God to do a work in your heart so that you never again have to give reluctantly or under compulsion, but only because you love him so much.

 ## For You and Your Kids

Preschool–Elementary

Make homemade cards or cookies and send them with grace-filled messages to people important to your children—relatives, teachers, baby-sitters, neighbors, and so on.

Middle–High School

Begin training your children to evaluate disappointments in light of the Lord's promise to work everything out for his own ends. How can they look at what happens as an opportunity from God to make a choice? When plans fall through, your sympathy will be welcomed, but also be sure to challenge them with, "How will you choose to handle this time that has just opened up to you? What opportunities does this change create for you?"

All Ages

Praise your kids when you see or hear that they've made the most of an unexpected opportunity by doing "good to all people" (Galatians 6:10). Talk about how the moment affected them as well as the other person(s) involved. Encourage each other to have sharp eyes for such moments.

session 6

rest for those he loves

For You Alone

Sabbath? Rest? Yeah, right!

For many, "Sabbath" has come to mean another twenty-four hours in which to get more done. You buzz around just as on any other day. Maybe your busyness looks different, and maybe you call it "low-key," but in all likelihood you spend at least part of the day fulfilling church commitments, running errands, cooking a big dinner, or completing tasks you can't seem to get done Monday through Friday. You think, *Now's the chance to get ahead, to clear the decks*—or at least your kitchen sink! But how often don't you fall into bed just as exhausted as any other night, already thinking about the busy week stretching out ahead of you?

The Hebrew word *šabbāt* means "rest." Though the Old Testament understanding of the word has to do not only with rest but worship, you'll focus primarily on *rest* during this session.

List every circumstance you can think of that prevents you from taking a regular Sabbath rest. Put a star next to the circumstances that are self-imposed (for example, cleaning your house) and a check mark next to those that are beyond your control (for example, your job requires you to work).

For You and God's Word

Most of you know that "Remember the Sabbath day by keeping it holy" (Exodus 20:8) is one of the Ten Commandments, along with "You shall have no other gods" and "You shall not murder" (Exodus 20:3, 13). What you may have forgotten is that this particular commandment gets more explanation—four verses—than any other on the list. Maybe the Lord knew it would be a particularly difficult commandment for his people to follow. Take a look at Exodus 20:8–11.

1. God begins by commanding his people to "remember" the Sabbath. What do you think it means to remember the Sabbath?

2. The purpose of remembering the Sabbath day is "to keep it holy." How does one go about keeping the Sabbath holy? What does it involve? What does it *not* involve?

3. Verse 10 outlines who should not work on the Sabbath. What is the reason given in verse 11 for not working?

4. Do you think Sabbath is (check all that apply)

    ❑   a necessity?

    ❑   an issue of preference?

    ❑   an apparent need?

    ❑   a command to be obeyed?

5. A wise, old farmer used to say, "You can get more work out of a team of horses in six days than in seven." Now, obviously you're not a team of horses, but how does this bit of wisdom relate to humans?

6. Why do you think God designed the Sabbath?

7. What are some possible consequences of failing to observe the Sabbath day?

8. Write down a plan to truly rest on a designated Sabbath day (it doesn't necessarily have to be Sunday) this coming week.

For You and Others

Jesus did not hesitate to heal on the Sabbath. From the disabled man lying near the pool at Bethesda (John 5:1–15) to the man with a shriveled hand (Luke 6:6–11) to the woman crippled for eighteen years (Luke 13:10–17), Jesus healed freely—and defended the healings to the critical Pharisees.

As a group, read Luke 13:10–17.

1. What was the synagogue ruler's disagreement with Jesus and what was the essence of his argument?

2. What was wrong with his reasoning?

3. Why do you think Jesus was not opposed to healing on the Sabbath when the Ten Commandments declared, "On it you shall not do any work" (Exodus 20:10)?

4. The woman Jesus healed was bent and couldn't stand up straight. She had been "crippled by a spirit" (verse 11). What lying spirit might be crippling you with the idea that resting on the Sabbath is not worth the effort?

5. What connections between the Sabbath, healing, and freedom do you see in this passage?

6. Commandments and laws set limitations on what you are allowed to do. How can you explain God's commandment to rest on the Sabbath day as a law that gives you freedom rather than restriction?

The theology of progress forces us to act before we are ready. We speak before we know what to say. We respond before we feel the truth of what we know. In the process, we inadvertently create suffering, heaping imprecision upon inaccuracy, until we are all buried under a mountain of misperception. But Sabbath says, Be still. Stop. There is no rush to get to the end, because we are never finished. Take time to rest, and eat, and drink, and be refreshed. And in the gentle rhythm of that refreshment, listen to the sound the heart makes as it speaks to the quiet truth of what is needed.

WAYNE MULLER, *SABBATH: RESTORING THE SACRED RHYTHM OF REST*

7. Discuss the ways in which a failure to keep the Sabbath may have created suffering for you, for your family, and for Christians in general.

8. How do you think keeping the Sabbath could alleviate the kind of suffering Wayne Muller writes about?

9. How could keeping the Sabbath alleviate other problems in life that cause suffering or illness — whether physical, spiritual or emotional?

10. "There is no rush to get to the end, because we are never finished." Does this observation encourage you or discourage you? Why?

The psalmist wrote, "In vain you rise early and stay up late, toiling for food to eat—for he grants sleep to those he loves" (Psalm 127:2).

11. The busy, active King Solomon of Israel wrote this psalm. What do you think he means in this verse?

12. Does this verse seem to advocate laziness or a lack of responsibility? Discuss.

13. As a group share the things that prevent you from getting good sleep—things like worries, physical disorders, children's sleeping patterns and illnesses, a demanding job. How could a deeper reliance on God's ability to care for you produce better sleep?

14. Close by praying with each other for the courage and strength to enter God's rest in spite of circumstances that would rob you of it.

 ## For You and God

You know when your children are tired. Certain behaviors tip you off to their need for a nap, an early bedtime, or perhaps a slower pace. In preparation for rest, you might pick them up, cuddle them, and sing in a rhythm that settles their spirits and causes tensions to fade. Is there anything more beautiful than a peacefully sleeping child? Your heavenly Father looks lovingly at you as you rest in him, at peace in his sovereignty.

Set aside a Sabbath day in which you can spend at least an hour alone with God. No agendas, no quiet time, no Bible study, no journaling, no nothing except a quiet hour in which you let his Sabbath rest seep deep into your spirit.

Imagine that you've been walking for six straight days, and your legs are weak. You need a break. "Abba, Daddy," you say to the Lord, "I'm tired." He gently smiles and says, "Yes, let's give you a break." And he squats down so that you can, with a tiny jump, hoist yourself up onto his back. You fit perfectly between his shoulder blades. You take comfort in the strength of his back, and you wrap your arms around his shoulders, your legs around his waist. You close your eyes, inhaling deeply. He supports you gently with his strong arms and rises, taking your weight on himself. You can rest—at peace, protected, and loved by your great and good Father.

Meditate on this Scripture in the coming week:

> Let the beloved of the Lord rest secure in him,
> for he shields him all day long,
> and the one the Lord loves
> rests between his shoulders.
>
> DEUTERONOMY 33:12

For You and Your Kids

Preschool–Elementary

One of the best things you can do to help your young children experience Sabbath in a positive way is to honor a Sabbath rest yourself. Your stress spills over onto your children; your peace does also. Change the tenor of your Sabbath day by modifying the pace of some activities: instead of watching TV while you pay bills, play a game together as a family; instead of encouraging rowdy play with the neighborhood kids, spend time together at a nearby park. Consider keeping a few special toys—low-key or family oriented—for Sabbath-only play.

Middle–High School

Busy, busy, busy! Chances are your kids are busier than ever with homework, sports events, youth group activities, volunteerism, part-time jobs, and social fun. Unfortunately, this busy phase of life comes just when your growing young adults—adolescents especially—need more sleep than ever. In spite of apparent impossibilities, consider a one-month Sabbath experiment. Pick one day each week in a coming month—it doesn't have to be the same day, depending on your family's schedule—and designate it as a day of rest. Reduce or eliminate as many commitments as possible on these days: homework, appointments, games or practices, chores, job hours. Kids this age may dig in their heels at the thought, but encourage them by setting a positive example with your own activities and by talking about how much you'll enjoy the chance to spend time with them. Choose slower, quieter activities for the day:

- Take a walk, perhaps somewhere you haven't gone before—on the beach, in an unfamiliar neighborhood, in a city park, along a country road. Make sure your pace is leisurely—this isn't the Stairmaster!

- Play board games.

- Read a book out loud together (something that interests all your children).

- Sing.

- Take a long ride in the car.

- Sit in the sun.

- Sit in the shade.

- Sit in front of the fireplace or a campfire.

- Talk together about past family events and good memories.

Use the time not just to rest but to enjoy the very special people who belong to your family. Take note of what's positive about the experiment and what's frustrating. Compare notes: What does your child like most about his weekly "day off"? What adjustments can you make so that the valuable aspects can be preserved?

All Ages

At least once a month, treat your Sabbath (again, it doesn't necessarily have to be a Sunday) like a family vacation. Plan it, protect it, and pull it off! Designate a specific day for rest. Go away if you have to, especially if your home is full of reminders of all the things you have to do. Get your kids' input on a restful plan for the day. You could keep the Sabbath according to Jewish practice—from sundown on one day to sundown the next. Decline commitments by explaining that your day is already full. Disconnect yourself from the need to be available to everyone and everything. Unplug your home phones, turn off your cell phones, and keep your computer shut down. Give yourself some grace to get in the habit: Sabbath can be torturous for those who can't sit still for even five minutes, and kids may cry, "Mom, I'm bored!" But as the busyness of our days pile up, this family discipline is one you won't regret keeping.

leader's notes

The following notations refer to the questions in the "For You and Others" in each Bible study session. The information included here is intended to give guidance to small group leaders.

session 1:
no time for bad feelings

Question 1. "The pattern of this world" can take two forms, depending on your outlook, background, and environment. For some, the pattern will take the form of laziness, doing only enough to make ends meet or keep a basic job. For others, following this world's ways will mean going all-out, giving 110 percent, putting all else aside in order to get ahead. Neither approach is biblical or advisable. A measured, Christ-centered approach to work is as important as any discipline in the Christian life.

Question 3. Paul saw the dangers inherent in living the way the world chooses to live. God's ways and the ways of the world often collide, as the passage in 1 Corinthians indicates. The wisdom of the world is foolishness in the eyes of the all-wise God.

Question 4. The transformation of the believer is a process. Our minds and hearts gradually become more and more in tune with the One we follow and serve.

Question 6. The more we become transformed, the more our minds grow in tune with Christ, the easier it will be, naturally and without hesitation, to discover and follow his will in our daily lives.

Question 9. The surest sign of an "orderly and responsible inner life" will be evidence of the Spirit's control in our lives. His fruit as described in Galatians 5:22–23 is evidence of his presence.

Question 10. Whenever we make the positive character trait more important than the work of God that produced it, we twist God's wisdom into the world's foolishness.

Question 11. Here's how the world evaluates success as a mother: raising children who are well behaved, have their hair combed, wear clean clothing, perhaps with name brands blazing on their tags, are involved in a variety of acceptable activities; maintaining a home that is well designed and decorated; driving a certain type of car. You can add to the list. All of these things are not evil in and of themselves, of course. However, the *motive* behind them—to "look" successful rather than to be what God has created you and your children to be—makes all the difference.

Question 12. It can help us determine which activities are important and which are not. Then, as we carefully schedule these activities, we find joy in accomplishing them and joy in the time we have for doing other things.

session 2:
everything's a priority!

Question 1. Human beings recognize that there is something beyond themselves, beyond their understanding of time as they know it.

Question 2. Very little. The very concept of time demands a progression—a beginning and an end. Eternity, however, has no such flow or progression, no beginning or end—it just *is*. Most humans have difficulty even beginning to grasp any sort of concept of eternity, as the writer notes in the latter part of verse 11. We know eternity exists, but we can't understand it.

Question 3. In the eternal perspective, will what you're stressed-out about right now have any impact? Or will it cease to matter already tomorrow? Thinking in longer terms of time, or even in terms of eternity, can put fresh perspective on today's occupations and preoccupations.

Question 5. In terms of four elements: (1) Be happy (attitude), (2) do good (activity), (3) eat and drink (sustenance), and (4) find satisfaction in work (purpose).

Question 7. Some people can look at life on its surface level and be pleased with what they find. They enjoy their life, they have plenty to do, they have enough to eat and drink, and they find purpose in their work. Others, however, whether due to a naturally introspective nature or a tendency toward melancholy, ponder the deep things of life and have difficulty enjoying the basic flow and goodness of life. These folks need a special grace from God to continue to examine life fully—to do otherwise would go against their nature—but also to enjoy life as God intended it (see John 10:10). So joy in life comes rather naturally for some but takes a bit of effort and conscious reliance on God for others.

Question 10. While to-do lists can be helpful, they have little impact on eternity. Their importance lies in how they relate to our knowledge of God and his purposes in our lives, our understanding of his work, and our part in his plan and work.

Question 11. A sense of oneness and purpose with him and his work. Only then will we find satisfaction and contentment in life.

session 3:
a season for every activity

Question 1.

- Genesis 37:12-24 <u>betrayal</u>
- Genesis 37:25-36 <u>slavery</u>
- Genesis 39:7-20 <u>imprisonment</u>
- Genesis 41:41-43 <u>success or power</u>

Question 5. *God was with Joseph* in each season, and Joseph responded faithfully to his presence and leading.

Question 7.

- Genesis 37:12-14—traveling to check on his brothers' well-being
- Genesis 39:4-6—in charge of all of Potiphar's household as well as all he owned
- Genesis 39:22-23—in charge of all prisoners
- Genesis 41:41—in charge of all Egypt

Question 10.

- Genesis 39:3—successful
- Genesis 39:9-10—resistant to temptation
- Genesis 40:12,18—able to interpret dreams
- Genesis 41:16—humble
- Genesis 41:39—wise and discerning
- Genesis 41:57—generous

session 4:
the importance of being earnest

Question 4. Not at all. However, our plans must *always* include God first, not ourselves and our own wishes. The writer of Proverbs says the wise person will plan ahead (14:15) and commit all of his or her plans to God (16:3). Only then will we know success as we chart our days and weeks.

Question 5. While making plans in themselves isn't a form of boasting, making *bold* plans involves something of an "I can do this myself" spirit that doesn't include God in the equation. This sort of planning is a form of boasting in ourselves and our own abilities rather than a reliance on God and his direction in our lives. For the believer, anything done without God's involvement is sin.

Question 6. We may know what we have planned for tomorrow, but we don't actually know what tomorrow will bring, much less what the weeks and months and years ahead will bring—which is exactly James's point: Our future is truly known only to God.

Question 7. A mist is something fragile, temporary, thin. It doesn't take much more than a tiny wisp of wind for it to disappear. Our lives are like that mist. In a brief second, all we have planned and dreamed can be gone.

Question 8. Though our responsibilities and tasks are real and important, in the eternal scheme of things they are small and fragile, exactly like a mist. Looking at ourselves as a mist can help us realize the importance of focusing on the things that have eternal significance (our children's happiness and delight in God, for instance) rather than on the things that will last only a few seconds or years (such as cleaning the floors or remodeling the bathroom).

Question 9. Surrendering all our plans to God's will and direction takes them out of our hands and puts them exactly where they belong—*in his.* Now we can focus not on what *we're* getting done or not getting done but on what *he* wants for our lives and calendars. His direction for our planning can help us focus on the significant rather than getting stressed-out about the day's undone tasks.

It could well be the single biggest stress reducer available to us—delighting in God and his plan for our to-do lists instead of on the momentary (like a mist) pleasure gained from checking one more thing off a list.

Question 10. When we find ourselves annoyed by an unexpected interruption, we can pause to ask, "Lord, are you presenting me with a more important task than the one I had planned. Is this perhaps a chance to practice patience?"

Question 13. The ant is prepared no matter what the season. Its cycles aren't governed by a Day-Timer, nor is it so laid-back about life that its essential work goes undone. Without thought or planning, it follows the instincts with which it was created.

Question 14. We're not ants, at least not on most days. And we're not governed totally by instinct, as is the ant. However, the lessons we can learn can help us realize that neither laziness nor frenzied productivity are what God intends for our lives.

session 5:
time is pregnant

Question 1. Others may interrupt our schedule or plans with true interruptions. But when *God* interrupts, it's always with an opportunity. The challenge is, of course, knowing who's doing the interrupting! The more in tune we are with God and the more we've given our plans and schedules over to him, the easier the distinction will become. Notice: not *easy,* just easier.

Question 3. The opportunities are God's way of giving us a chance to influence others—our children, our husbands, our friends, our neighbors, the clerk in the grocery store—for good. We may think the extra few seconds or minutes we take with someone has little value, but God has a different way of measuring.

Question 6. God graciously measures our giving simply *by the act itself,* not by its amount or extent or extravagance. A gift of several seconds in a busy day is as important to God as the offering of a whole day to help someone in need.

Question 7. We tend to measure giving by the level of time, money, effort or whatever it is that is expended. We also tend to measure our giving in relationship to others: How does my giving measure up against her giving?

session 6:
rest for those he loves

Question 1. He couldn't tolerate the fact that Jesus healed on the Sabbath. He thought Jesus had plenty of time to do his healing "work" on the other six days of the week.

Question 2. He had so narrowly defined "work" that even a gift of helping someone in need was designated work and therefore was not to be allowed on the Sabbath.

Question 3. Jesus used the ruler's own rules to prove him wrong. If they could water their animals on the Sabbath, judging that "work" to be permissible because it was necessary and humane, how much more the "work" of healing this crippled woman. Jesus knew the true meaning of Sabbath rest. God's command to rest on the Sabbath wasn't meant to constrict but to free.

Question 5. The Sabbath was designed to give rest, which promotes healing, which gives us freedom to move throughout our week in a healthy and happy way.

Question 6. License to laze about—what a wonderful prospect! In our ever-moving, ever-doing culture, the command of God to rest on the Sabbath gives us freedom to *not* do the ordinary, everyday things that exhaust us. The Sabbath is not about restricting us, but about allowing us to revive our bodies and refresh our spirits.

Question 8. This is a suffering of the body and the spirit. The body becomes malnourished from not getting enough rest. The spirit is impoverished by too much frenzied activity and failing to spend time in refreshing and serene rest.

Question 9. Rest for the body and the spirit have been shown to produce a more harmonious blending of our physical, spiritual, and emotional aspects. "Downtime" or simple and pleasurable relaxation can heal illnesses that no medicine can cure.

Question 11. Solomon knew the tendency (perhaps because it was his own) to get so caught up in the producing that we lose a sense of the wholeness of life and of God's role in giving and sustaining life. He is speaking here about a "hurry up and get it all done" self-reliance rather than a reliance on God.

Question 12. It's all about *balance.* The Bible urges us to work hard (see the woman of Proverbs 31, for example), and it also urges us to take it easy (Exodus 20:5, God's command to rest). What Solomon wanted his readers to understand was that *it's all about relying on God.* When we're so absorbed by our work and busyness, we're usually out of tune with God, and all our work is empty—meaningless, even. When we're in tune with God, he'll help us balance both our work and our rest requirements, and he'll provide for our needs in the process.

A Mom's Ordinary Day

Jean E. Syswerda, General Editor

The eight Bible studies in this series are designed specifically to help a mom find wisdom from God's Word as she seeks to be the best mom, person, and disciple she can be.

Each study contains six sessions divided into five flexible portions: For You Alone, For You and God's Word, For You and Others, For You and God, and For You and Your Kids. The last section helps moms share each week's nugget of truth with their children.

Finding Joy in All You Are helps moms discover who they are as a whole person. Everyone wants a piece of mom, but this study will help a mom discover more about herself—as a mom, a believer, and a unique creation of God.

Gaining and Being a Friend takes an in-depth look at the various kinds of friendships, as well as how to be a better friend.

Growing Strong with God encourages moms to focus on cultivating their own spiritual lives.

Mothering without Guilt identifies and debunks the "perfect mom" stereotypes and encourages moms to be real—not perfect—and forgiven—not overcome by guilt.

Making Praise a Priority challenges moms to live their lives with their hands raised in praise rather than their heads hung in discouragement.

Managing Your Time gives a fresh biblical perspective on time and on what is important and worth cherishing.

Entering God's Presence covers the topic of prayer—everything from the joy of having access to God to the challenges of unanswered prayers.

Winning over Worry provides biblical teaching on the dead end of worry and the peace-promoting route of prayer.

Softcover
Finding Joy in All You Are 0-310-24712-8
Gaining and Being a Friend 0-310-24713-6
Growing Strong with God 0-310-24714-4
Mothering without Guilt 0-310-24715-2

Making Praise a Priority 0-310-24716-0
Managing Your Time 0-310-24717-9
Entering God's Presence 0-310-24718-7
Winning over Worry 0-310-24719-5

Pick up a copy at your favorite bookstore!

GRAND RAPIDS, MICHIGAN 49530 USA
WWW.ZONDERVAN.COM